Dedicated to the humanity of
Emmett, Martin,* Tamir, Trayvon, LaQuan, Eric, Michael,
Freddie, and the countless others.

* Yes, that Martin. Lest we forget that the life of Martin Luther King, Jr. was cut short when he was assasinated at the Loraine Motel

For Myles, Christian, Little J., Little B., Trip, Ali, S.J., Tyree and all of the
little black boys that bring me joy. May you never forget what great stock you come from.
And for the little black girls that love them Asha, Anya, Aniyah, Brianna, Chanlyr, Kyndal,
Brooklyn, and Laylah.
-VMR

For my Mom and Dad who always encouraged me to create.
And for my sister, Jori, who encourages me to do great things for all the brown creators that
continue to inspire and are inspired.
- C. T.

Text © 2017 Valerie M. Reynolds
Illustrations© 2017 Chris Turner/Hurston Media Group, LLC
www.joyofbeingablackboy.com

Author/Editor: Valerie M. Reynolds
Illustrator/Designer/Art Director: Chris Turner

Hᵐg

Hurston Media Group, LLC
1507 E. 53rd Street, Suite 196
Chicago, IL, 60615
www.hurstonmediagroup.com

ISBN Hardbook: 978-0-692-84726-8

Library of Congress Control Number
2 0 1 7 9 0 2 9 0 8

The Joys of Being a Little Black Boy

by Valerie M. Reynolds

Illustrated by Chris Turner

Hi, my name is Roy, and I live in one of the best cities in the world – Chicago, Illinois.

This is my pretty mama.

She says Chicago is the best because it's the home of the first black president, President Barack Obama.

And this here is my dad. His name is Roy, too.
He's a doctor who helps take care of me and you.

When he was a boy, he wanted to be like Charles Drew,
a black doctor who blazed a trail in blood transfusion.

Yep, it's true.

"Excellence of performance will transcend artificial barriers created by man."
- Dr. Charles Drew

Today is going to be so cool,
because I am part of an assembly at my school.

We get to talk about who we are today.
And here is what I am going to say:

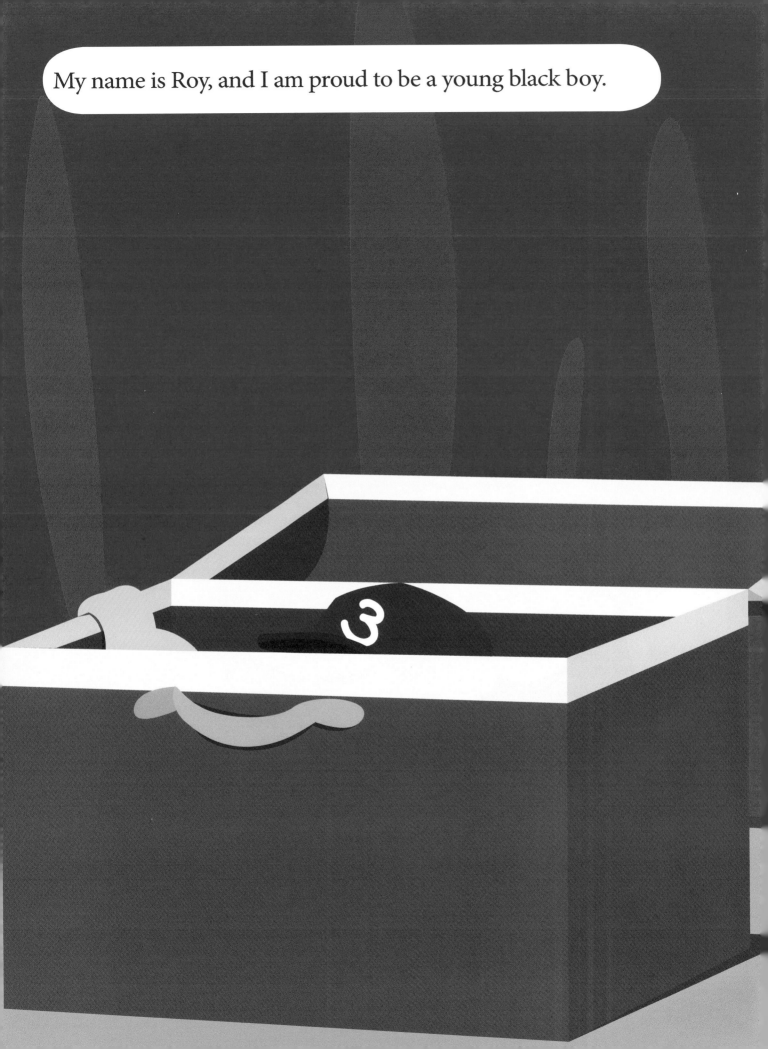

There are a lot of men who started out as a boy like me.
Their strength and courage is, no doubt, what set me free.

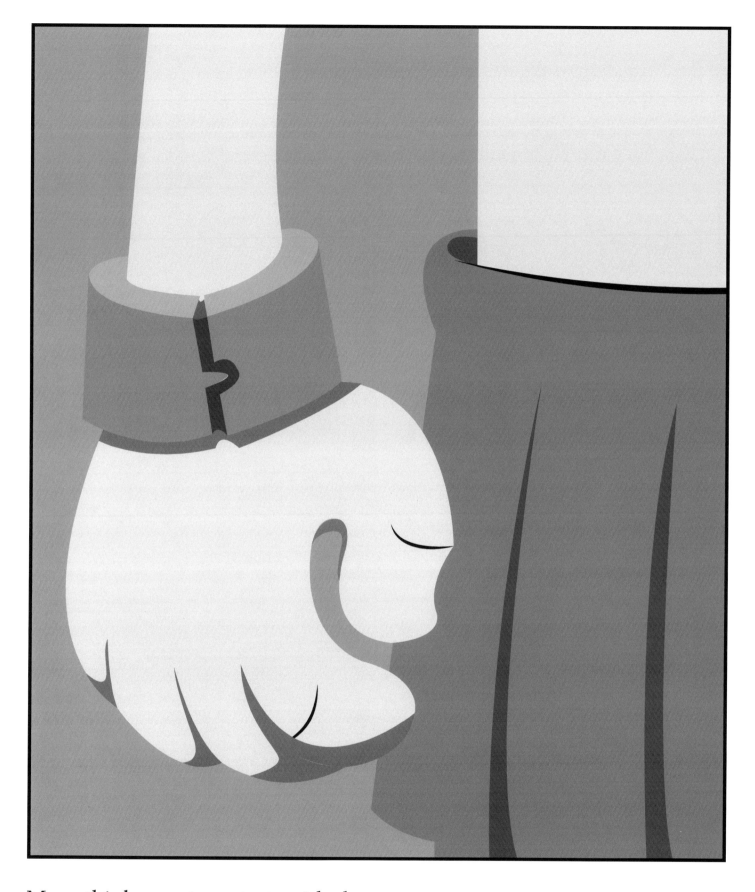

Many think our story starts with slavery.
But really, it starts in Africa with royalty and bravery.

The "boy king of Egypt" became king when he was just nine.

That's how old I am! Doesn't that blow your mind!

So when they tell you that our history starts as slaves, that's a decoy.

King Tut's reign proves there's power in being a young black boy.

Did you know that a free black man founded this great city?

His name is Jean Baptiste Point Du Sable. It's in the books, though that part is itty-bitty.

Frederick Douglass was a boy slave who taught himself how to write and read.

Se, back then it was against the law for blacks to know how to read, no matter how much one might beg and plead.

HOPE

THE
AUDACITY
OF
HOPE

So the next time you're reading a book, don't play coy.

Read loud and read proud. This is yet another great joy of being a young black boy.

Langston Hughes was a great writer who reminded us that life will be no crystal stair.

And that we must keep on pushing forward and choose not to despair.

So when your days are filled with little sisters, homework, and other things that annoy.

Remember that for us – my friends –these should be joys of being free black boys.

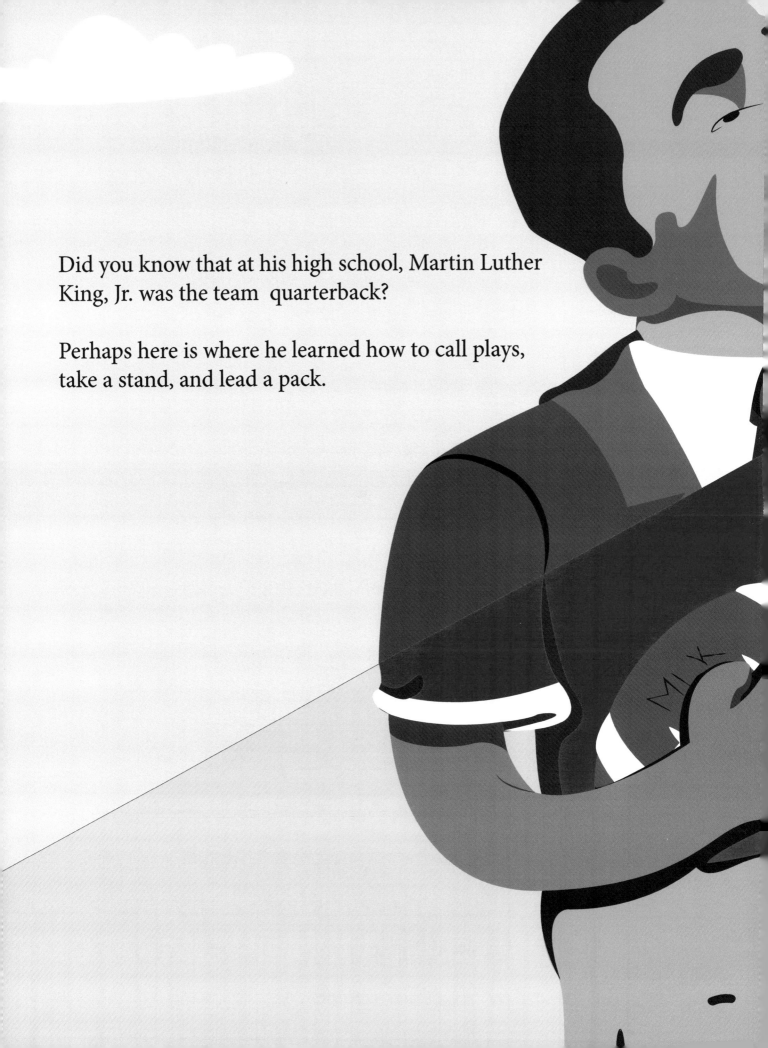

Did you know that at his high school, Martin Luther
King, Jr. was the team quarterback?

Perhaps here is where he learned how to call plays,
take a stand, and lead a pack.

So, when you're outside throwing that ball, remember it is more than just a toy.

This is the joy of being a young black boy.

The next time you find yourself feeling low, stand tall and enjoy.

Malcolm taught us the strength, pride, and beauty in being a young black boy.

Have you heard of the world's
greatest boxer, Muhammad Ali,
or you may know him as Cassius
Clay?

He wasn't the greatest just
because he could fight,
but because he stood
up and made the world
hear what he had to say.

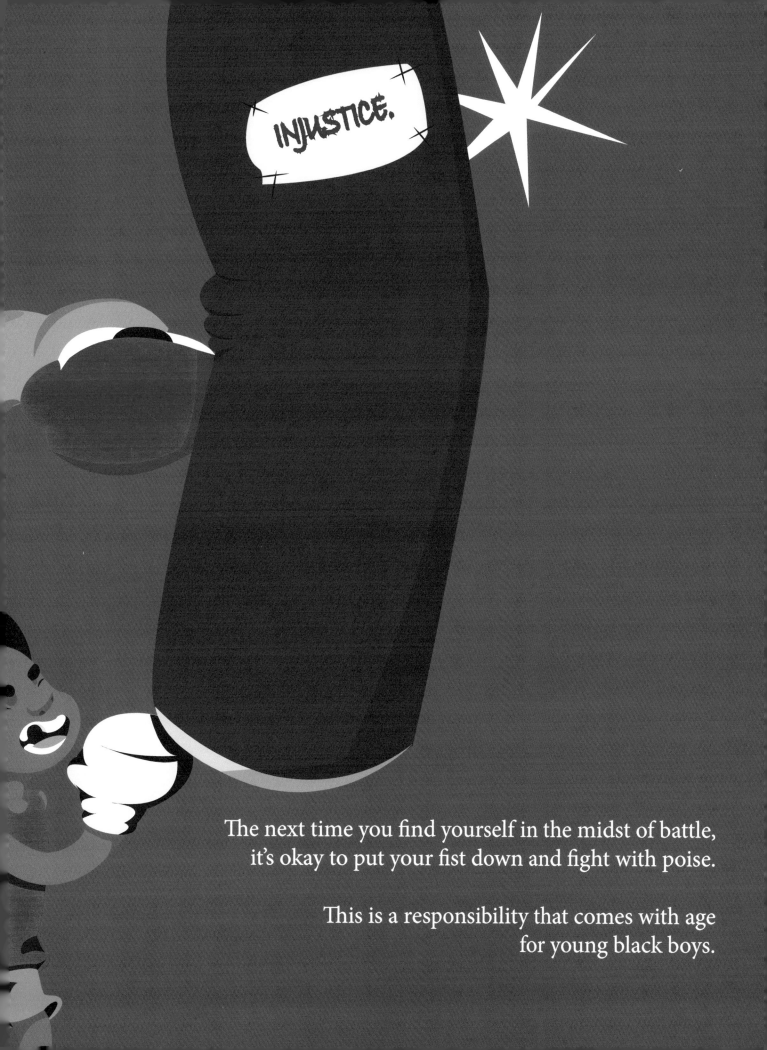

The next time you find yourself in the midst of battle, it's okay to put your fist down and fight with poise.

This is a responsibility that comes with age for young black boys.

After graduating high school, Colin Powell joined the ROTC.

When he did this, becoming the first black Secretary of State is something he never thought he'd be.

So when you start to work, don't think of it as a job that just employs.

These are the first steps to take in making powerful black men out of playful young boys.

CHAMPIONS!:

Like our boys from Jackie Robinson West, maybe I can play in the Little League World Series one day.

I hope to play as good as them, or maybe be as good as Mo'ne.

Though some used tactics that tried to destroy,
I remember the day they won and the whole world
saw the joy in being a young black boy.

Does the name Madiba ring a bell? It's another name for Nelson Mandela, who spent almost 27 years in jail.

No, not for doing anything wrong. But fighting for justice and standing strong.

You see, belief and resistance is sort of how our freedom has been alloyed. Mandela ended up becoming President of South Africa, that makes me even prouder to be a young black boy.

So many people are frightened by who we are.
That's because they know our ancestors planted
the seeds for us to grow wide and far.

But I am here to tell you,
that what's in our DNA cannot be destroyed.

And though it may not always be easy,
there is true joy in being a young black boy.

Parent/Teacher Guide

President Barack Obama (August 4, 1961—)

Barack Obama was the 44th president of the United States of America. He is the country's first black president. He was born on August 4, 1961 in Honolulu, Hawaii and spent much of his childhood there. He received a B.A in political science from Columbia University and then entered Harvard Law School, where he was elected the first black editor of the *Harvard Law Review*. After graduating from Harvard, he moved to Chicago to work as a community organizer on Chicago's far south side, where he met his wife, Michelle, a Princeton Law graduate. Mrs. Obama was born and raised on Chicago's South Side and attended Whitney Young High School. Together, they have two daughters - Sasha and Malia.

Charles Drew (June 3, 1904 - April 1, 1950)

Charles Drew is the creator and founder of what is today referred to as a "blood bank." Because many states in the U.S. did not accept black men and women into their schools, he attended medical school in Montreal, Canda. While teaching at the medical school at Howard University, he received a fellowship to lead the research that developed a method for processing and preserving blood plasma. This research was later used as the topic of the thesis that earned him a Doctorate of Medical Science degree from Columbia University; becoming the first black person to ever receive a doctorate from Columbia. Drew later became the Director of the Red Cross Blood Program. In this role, he called a press confernece to state that there was no scientific or biologic need to "segregate" blood based on race. He later quit the Red Cross because of the military's practice to separate blood from black and white solders.

American Slavery (1581 - 1863)

Slavery was a United Staes policy that imprisoned Africans and Black Americans; forcing them to work in inhumane conditions with no pay. As slaves, black men, women and children endured murderous and brutal conditions as they tended to farms and homes, built some of the country's most historic buildings and monuments, and often-times cared for the very men and women who abused and staked "ownership" of them. Though this was a dark and painful period for black people, black slaves stayed strong and fought for their freedom. Many of today's leaders - including many in this book - took inspiration from the fact that if their ancestors could make it through slavery then they could make it through anything....and so can you.

Tutankhamun (also known as "King Tut")

Known as the "boy king of Egypt," King Tut reigned as Pharoh of Egypt for eight to nine years. Born circa 1341 B.C.E., he was given the name Tutankhaten. He later changed his name to Tutankhamun, which means "the living image of Amun." King Tut assumed the throne of pharoh (or king) when he was only nine years old. It is not exactly known how King Tut died, but he only ruled as pharoah for approximately 10 years. He died at the age of 19, some time aroud 1324. His in-tact tomb was discovered by archaeologist Howard Carter on Nov, 4, 1922. This day is now known as King Tut Day. Egypt is one of 54 countries located in Africa, the world's second largest continent.

Jean Baptiste Point du Sable (1745? - Aug. 28, 1818)

DuSable was born a free, black Frenchman in St. Dominique (now known as Haiti) in ~1745. He is the founder of Chicago; settling sometime in the 1770s in the area that is now called "the bank of the Chicago River." DuSable was an aspiring entrepreneur, who, as a polyglot - a person that speaks many langauges - became a lucrative business man; growing his plot of 30 acres into a thriving trading post of approximately 800 acres in just a few years. His trading post included a garden, a dairy mill, a bakery, a smokehouse, a horse stable, and living quarters for his employees. DuSable was also a fur trapper and trader with an official license from the British government. He married a Native American woman named Kittihawa in 1778; together, they had a son and daughter. After selling his estate in 1800, DuSable settled in Peoria, Il. He died on August 28, 1818 in St. Charles, MO.

Langston Hughes (February 1, 1902-May 22, 1967)

Born James Mercer Langston Hughes in 1902, Hughes was an American writer whose vibrant, true-to-life depictions of Black Americans are largely affiliated with the movement that became known as the Harlem Renaissance. Although Hughes is most popularly known as a poet, he also wrote many novels, plays and short stories. His first, and one of his most famous poems, "The Negro Speaks of Rivers", was published in 1921 less than one year after he graduated high school. In 1940, Hughes began writing a column for the *Chicago Defender*, a black newspaper that played a major role in the "Great Migration" of blacks from the Jim Crow South to the north. Hughes died in 1967 in New York City.

Dr. Martin Luther King, Jr (January 15, 1929 - April 4, 1968)

Known to many as the pre-eminent leader of the Civil Rights Movement, Dr. Martin Luther King, Jr. was born Michael King, Jr. in Atalanta, GA. King's father later changed both of their names from Micheal to Martin Luther in honor of the theologian who led Europe's Protestant Reformation. Dr. King was an accomplished student; graduating from high school at the age of fifteen. In addition to serving as co-pastor of Ebenezer Baptist Chruch in Atlanta, King received his Bachelor of Arts degree from Morehouse College and his PhD from Boston University in 1955. He played a leading role in ending legal segregation and also contributed significantly to the creation of the Civil Rights Act of 1964 and the Voting Rights Act of 1965. King received the Nobel Peace Prize in 1964. He was assassinated on April 4, 1968 at the Lorraine Motel in Memphis, TN.

Malcolm X (May 19, 1925 - February 21, 1965)

Born Malcolm Little in Omaha, NE, Malcolm X was an outspoken activitst who spoke honestly and eloquently of the atrocities of historic, racial segregation. Malcom dropped his last name, Little, referring to it as the name given to his ancestors by their slave owners, and replaced it with X to symbolize his true African name that had been lost in slavery. He is often accredited with the exponential growth and visibility of the Nation of Islam. Malcolm X was extremly vocal about how institutionalized racism, fueled by white supremecy, worked in deliberation to suppress the economic and societal growth of blacks. Malcolm X was killed by three assiailants in 1965 while speaking at the Audubon Ballroom in Manhattan, New York.

Muhammad Ali (January 17, 1942 - June 3, 2016)

A world-renowned prizefighter, Muhammad Ali was born Cassius Clay in Louisville, KY and won a gold medal in boxing at the 1960 Olympics. After being refused service at a white restaurant, he threw his gold medal into the Ohio River to protest the United States' treatment of blacks. In 1964, he officially changed his name to Muhammad Ali, shedding what he referred to as his "slave name." Ali is also known for refusing military service when, in 1967, he refused to enlist in the Vietnam war. "My conscience won't let me go shoot my brother, or some darker people, or some poor, hungry people... They never called me nigger, they never lynched me, they didn't put no dogs on me…," he said speaking of why he would refuse to fight in the war. Ali - affectionately referred to as "the Champ"- was diagnosed with Parkinson's Disease in 1984, and after a valiant, 32-year-battle against the degenerative disease, "the Champ" died in June of 2016.

Colin Powell (April 5, 1937—)

Born in Harlem and raised in the Bronx, Colin Powell is a retired four-star general in the United States Army, the first black Secretary of State, and the first - and so far the only - black man to serve on the Joint Chiefs of Staff; where he also served as the Chairman. After graduating high school, Powell enrolled in City College of New York, where he joined the ROTC. Upon graduation, Powell was commissioned as a second lieutenant in the U.S. Army, where he climbed through the ranks with an extensive military career that includes two tours in Vietnam, obtaining a staff postion at the Pentagon, a promotion to Brigadier General in 1976, and becoming the national security advisor in 1987. He was appointed as the U.S. Secretary of State on January 20, 2001.

Jackie Robinson West/Mo'ne Davis

Named in honor of the country's first black man to play major league professional baseball, Jackie Robinson West (JRW) was a Little Leage baseball team from Chicago's South Side. They captivated the world with a phenomenal run during the 2014 Little League World Series, winning the Little League U.S title* but graciously falling short of the world championship when losing to the Seoul Little League team of Seoul, South Korea. Mo'ne Davis is a breakout pitcher also from the 2014 Little League World Series. She is from Philadelphia, PA and during the Series, she became the first female pitcher to win and pitch a shutout in the history of the Little League World Series.
*In 2015, JRW was stripped of its title as a result of rule violations commited by league officials

Nelson Mandela (July 18, 1918 - December 5, 2013)

Born in the Xhosa tribe of South Africa, Nelson Mandela was elected as the first black President of South Africa in 1994. He was also South Africa's first black head of state. Before being elected as president, he was a South African activist who fought against the racial discrimination of apartheid – South Africa's formal system of racial classification and segregation. As a result of his activism against apartheid, in 1962 Mandela was arrested. After what became known as the Rivonia Trial, he was sentenced to life in prison and spent 27 years in jail. On Feb. 11, 1990 Mandela was released from prison and Apartheid officially ended in 1994. Nelson Mandela died on December 5, 2013 at the age of 95.